See for yourself

THE STREET

Jeff Stanfield

WAYLAND

Homes • Shops • School • The Street • Transport

HOW TO USE THIS BOOK

This book will help you find out all about streets. All the questions highlighted in **bold** have answers on pages 26–27, but try to work them out for yourself, first. Investigate your own streets by trying some of the detective activities on pages 28–29. You'll find difficult words explained on page 30.

All the photographs in this book were taken in Edinburgh. So you can compare the streets in Edinburgh to your own streets.

Series and book editor: Polly Goodman
Book designer: Jean Wheeler
Cover design: Dome Design

First published in 1997 by Wayland Publishers Ltd
61 Western Road, Hove, East Sussex BN3 1JD, England

This paperback edition first published in 1999.

© Copyright 1997 Wayland Publishers Ltd

British Library Cataloguing in Publication Data
Stanfield, Jeff
   The Street. – (See For Yourself)
   1. Cities and towns – Scotland – Edinburgh –
   Juvenile literature
   I. Title
   307.7'6'094134

ISBN 0 7502 2522 X

Photographic credits:
All photographs, except the following, were taken by Angus Blackburn.
Cover (centre): Tony Stone Worldwide; *cover (bottom left)*: British Telecommunications PLC; *cover (top left & back)*: Wayland Picture Library; *page 9 (bottom)*: British Telecommunications PLC.

Typeset by Jean Wheeler, England
Printed and bound in Italy by G. Canale & C.S.p.A.

CONTENTS

STREET NAMES

Most streets have names. What is the name of your street?

Some streets are named after buildings, such as Station Road or School Street.

▼ **Can you think of a name for this street?**

Other streets are named after jobs that people do.

Look at this shop. ▶

What would you call this street?

◀ Some streets are named after places, like the street on the left.

Are there any streets near you that are named after places?

POST BOXES

Most post boxes are red so they can be seen easily on the street.

This boy is posting a letter in ▶ a post box called a pillar box.

◀ Look at the post box on the corner of Grange Road.

How is it different from the pillar box?

All post boxes have a  white panel on them, like this one.

What information does the panel give to people about posting their letters?

Every post box also has a crown on the front. The crown can be gold or red. It shows that the post is run by the Royal Mail.

◀ This postman is collecting letters from the post box.

What will happen to the letters now?

TELEPHONES

Not all telephone boxes look the same.

◀ This is an older, red telephone box. There are not so many of these left nowadays.

These are much newer telephone boxes. ▶

How are they different from the red box?

8

◀ This new telephone box looks different from the other new ones. This is because it is owned by a different company.

The other boxes are owned by British Telecom. This box is owned by Interphone.

This telephone box ▶ has no door. Disabled people can use this type of box more easily.

Can you think of the different reasons why people might need to use a telephone box?

STREET MACHINES

Machines are usually found in streets near town or city centres.

Are there any machines like these in your street?

▲ This machine is a cashpoint.

People can get money from cashpoints using a special card with their own code.

Do you know how the code is entered into the machine?

This is a parking meter. It is ▶ beside a parking space at the side of the street.

When money is put into the parking meter, the dial at the top moves. The dial shows the amount of time you are allowed to park your car.

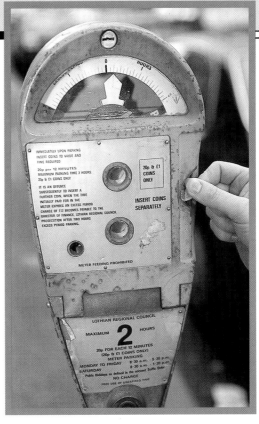

◀ This is a machine for buying train tickets. It is in a train station.

Why do you think this machine is useful for people who are in a rush?

STREET LAMPS

Street lamps light up the roads and pavements when it is dark.

Why do you think this is helpful?

This is an old, Victorian gas lamp. ▶ In Victorian times, people called lamplighters used to walk round and light them every evening.

◀ Here is a modern street lamp.

How is it different from the older gas lamp?

▲ These are road lamps. They are much taller than the pavement lamps.

Why do you think they have two arms and lamps?

This blue, modern street ▶ lamp has been designed to look attractive.

Why do you think this is?

SIGNS AND MARKINGS

Street signs are usually on upright, metal posts, or written on the road.

◀ These yellow markings are outside a school. They say SCHOOL KEEP CLEAR.

Why should drivers not park here?

▼ Only buses can stop here.

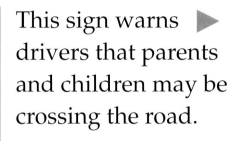

This sign warns ▶ drivers that parents and children may be crossing the road.

◀ People must not drive faster than 30 miles per hour on this road.

Only cyclists ▶ should use this street.

For ¹₂ mile

◀ **What do you think this sign warns drivers about?**

What signs or markings do you have in your street?

STREET CROSSINGS

Crossing busy streets can be tricky. Some streets have special crossings to help us. Remember to always use the Green Cross Code when crossing the road.

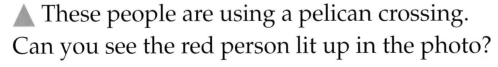

▲ These people are using a pelican crossing. Can you see the red person lit up in the photo?

Do you know what it means and what the people are waiting for?

▶ This is a zebra crossing. There are no traffic lights on a zebra crossing, but traffic has to stop if people are on the crossing.

What are the differences between the pelican crossing and the zebra crossing?

◀ These people are crossing the street with the help of a school crossing patrol lady.

Why do you think she is wearing a bright coat? Who do you think her sign is for?

UNDER THE STREET

Pipes and cables under the street bring services such as gas, water and electricity to our homes.

◀ These men are laying new pipes. When they have finished, the hole will be filled and the road mended.

Why do you think cones are put around the hole?

Metal covers like these show what is under the street.

What do ▶
you think
is under
this cover?

▲ Firemen and women get water for their hoses from under this cover.

▼ Drains like this help rainwater run off the street, which stops flooding.

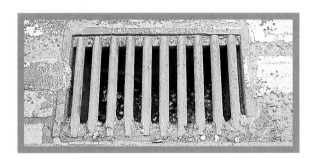

This worker is going under the street. He is held to a lift by a metal rope. ▶

Why do you think he is wearing
a hard hat, waterproof suit and
carrying an air supply?

WORK IN THE STREET

There are many different types of work in the street.

Very busy streets often need repairing because the cars, lorries and buses that travel on them make them crack. Street repairs are called road-works.

▲ These workers are repairing the road surface.

What do you think will happen to the traffic near here?

Some people's jobs are delivering to houses in the street

This lady is delivering milk.  Does anyone deliver anything to your home, or to other homes near yours?

▲ Police officers work on the street, either on foot, in cars or on horses.

How might police officers help people in the street?

SPECIAL STREETS

Some streets are just for certain types of transport.

◀ This street has a cycle lane on each side. They are just for cyclists.

How are the cycle lanes separated from the traffic lanes?

These are a different ▶ type of cycle lane.

They have their own traffic lights. They are completely separate from roads with traffic on them.

▲ Town and city-centre streets are often busy, so there may be special lanes just for buses.

How do you think bus lanes make it easier for buses to run on time?

Some streets, like this one, ▶ are just for people on foot. They are called pedestrian zones. No vehicles are allowed in pedestrian zones.

Why do you think there are pedestrian zones in towns and cities?

KEEPING STREETS TIDY

Streets need to be kept tidy.

This man is cleaning the ▶
pavement using a sweeper.
The machine is very modern.

**How else are our pavements
kept clean?**

◀ This road sweeper keeps the
gutters clear of litter and leaves.
If the gutters are not cleared,
rainwater cannot reach the drains
and the gutters look untidy.

**What could happen to the
streets if the gutters and drains
are blocked?**

◀ We can help keep the streets tidy by putting our litter in bins like this one.

This is a different type of bin. ▶

What do you think this bin is for?

ANSWERS TO QUESTIONS

Pages 4–5 Street Names

You could name this street Castle Street or Grave Street because there is a castle and graves beside it.

The street could be called Baker Street.

Pages 6–7 Post Boxes

The post box in Grange Road is not round like the pillar box. It is rectangular and is set into the wall.

The white panel shows the times that the letters are collected from the box.

The letters will be sorted. Some will be local. Others will be sent further away, or even abroad. Then they will all be delivered to the addresses written on the envelopes.

Pages 8–9 Telephone Boxes

The new telephone boxes have more windows so there is more light inside. They have gaps at the bottom so that litter does not collect in the boxes.

People use telephone boxes if they are away from home, or if they don't have a telephone in their own home. In an emergency, phone boxes are used to call the fire brigade, the ambulance service or the police by dialling 999.

Pages 10–11 Street Machines

The code is entered into the cashpoint machine by pressing the buttons below the screen.

People in a rush can buy their ticket from a machine without having to queue in the ticket office.

Pages 12–13 Street Lamps

Street lamps make it easier to see other people, cyclists and cars coming.

The new lamp is taller and has less decoration than the Victorian one. It has a bigger lamp because it was designed for an electric light.

Since these road lamps are for a dual carriageway, they have two arms and lamps to light both sides of the road.

The blue lamp was designed to look attractive because it is outside a café, where people sit and have a drink.

Pages 14–15 Signs and Markings

Cars should not park outside schools so that children and drivers can see each other clearly.

This sign warns drivers the road may be slippery for $1/2$ mile.

Pages 16–17 Street Crossings

The red-lit person means it is not safe to cross. When it turns to green and an alarm sounds, it is safe to cross.

You don't have to press any buttons or wait for any lights on a zebra crossing. But you do have to check that traffic has stopped before you cross.
       The pelican crossing is electronic. You must press a button and wait for the green person to light before you cross. You must look out for traffic in a certain direction. The marking on the road tells you this.

The bright coat means that drivers can see the school crossing patrol clearly. Her sign is for motorists. It tells them to stop.

Pages 18–19 Under the Street

Cones warn pedestrians and drivers of road-works in the street.

Under this cover there is a gas tap. Gas workers use it to turn the gas on and off.

The hard hat, waterproof clothing and air supply are for safety. The worker is also carrying a torch and a radio for safety.

Pages 20–21 Work in the Street

Road-works often cause traffic jams by making roads one-way or using traffic lights. Sometimes streets are closed while they are repaired.

Police officers help to stop crime, give people directions, look after people hurt in accidents and direct traffic.

Pages 22–23 Special Streets

The cycle lanes are coloured red with white dashes along the side to separate them from the traffic lanes. No cars are allowed on the cycle lanes.

Bus lanes make it easier for buses to run on time because buses are not held up behind other traffic.

Pedestrian zones are safer areas for people to walk since they do not have any traffic. They are also attractive places for people to sit and have a drink in a pavement café, like the one in the picture.

Pages 24–25 Keeping Street Tidy

Streets are also kept clean with brooms and bins on wheels. Litter bins are for putting rubbish into.

If the gutters and drains are blocked, rainwater will not be able to escape and the street could flood.

The red bin is for dog's mess.

DETECTIVE ACTIVITIES

It can be lots of fun investigating streets. Why not become a street detective and try some of the activities below with the help of an adult.

● Some children from a school in Australia have written to you. They want to know what the street you live in is like. What would you tell them?

● Streets have great noises. Different streets have different sounds. Collect the sounds of your street on a tape. Which are your favourite sounds?

● Find streets that are named after buildings, jobs, places and people near you.

● Draw pictures of some different street signs that you find near your home.

● Make a drawing of a post box near your home. Don't forget to add labels to your drawing about the different parts of the post box. Draw a picture map of the way to it from your home.

● Post boxes tell people posting letters lots of things. What does your local post box tell you?

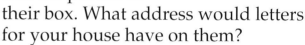

● Go to your nearest post office and find out what happens to letters that are posted in their box. What address would letters for your house have on them?

● How many different types of telephone boxes can you find in your local area? Draw pictures of them. Can you put them into age order?

● What street machines does your family use?

● Hunt for street lights near your home. Draw pictures of the different lights you find.

● Draw some of the street signs in your local area. Add labels to say what they mean.

● Draw a plan of the road outside your school. Mark on it the street markings. What do the markings tell people?

● You have been asked to tell some nursery children how to use a pelican crossing. What would you say to them? Use page 16 to help you.

● Streets are often changing. Are there any changes taking place in your street today?

● How has your street changed since you can remember?

● Draw pictures, or make a list of people you see working in your street today.

● What special streets have you got in your local area?

● Write down two lists of words: one of things you like about your street, and the other about things you don't like.

● Make a calendar of what's happening in your street for a week.

● How have people tried to keep streets in your area tidy and attractive?

● What would you do to make your street better for children of your age?

DIFFICULT WORDS

Air supply Artificial air in a container, used by people going where there is a lack of air, such as firemen going into a fire, or people going underground.

School crossing patrol A person who sees children safely across the road outside schools. They carry a large, round sign on a pole which tells the traffic to stop so children can cross the road safely.

Bus lane A special road, or part of a road, which only buses can use.

Cables Special wires that electricity and telephone messages are carried through. They are either underground or hung in the air between poles.

Cycle lanes Special roads, or parts of roads, that only cyclists can use.

Drains Holes in the ground that rainwater runs into.

Gas lamp Over 100 years ago, the streets were lit by gas lamps. Lamplighters walked around each evening to light them, and in the morning to put them out.

Green Cross Code A code you should always use when crossing the road: 1. Find a safe place to cross. 2. Stand on the pavement and look and listen all round for traffic. 3. If traffic is coming, let it pass. Look all round again. 4. When there is no traffic near, walk straight across, looking and listening while you cross.

Gutters The side of the road next to the pavement. Rainwater often rushes along the gutters heading for drains.

Litter Rubbish, such as sweet papers and cans that are dropped.

Pillar box A type of post box, shaped like a pillar.

Pelican crossing A crossing where people push a button to operate traffic lights, which stop the traffic.

Traffic Moving vehicles, such as cars and lorries.

Waterproof suit Clothing that water cannot get into.

Zebra crossing A crossing marked by black and white stripes over the road. When people step on to the crossing, the traffic must stop.

Victorian The time when Queen Victoria ruled Britain, from 1837–1901.

Other Books to Read

Going Places: Finding The Way by Barbara Taylor (A&C Black, 1995)
History From Objects In The Street by Karen Bryant-Mole (Wayland, 1994)
History Mysteries: In The Street by Gill Tanner and Tim Wood
  (A&C Black, 1996)
Look Out On the Road by Paul Humphries (Evans, 1994)
Maps and Journeys by Kate Petty (A&C Black, 1993)
Mapwork 1 by David Flint and Mandy Suhr (Wayland, 1992)
Mapwork 2 by Julie Warne and Mandy Suhr (Wayland, 1992)
Take Care on the Road by Carole Wale (Wayland, 1996)
Streets In Victorian Times by Richard Wood (Wayland, 1996)

You can find more about streets in your area by visiting a local library or museum and looking at maps and photographs.

INDEX

Page numbers in **bold** show that there is a photograph aswell as information.